Worldwide
Creativity
Mindfulness

This journal belongs to:

_____

and

_____

About the Author

Worldwide Creativity Mindfulness is a family business born out of the desire to help children develop, giving them the opportunity to know themselves, offering them personal development activities, and helping them nurture deeper bonds with family, all while finding greater joy, happiness, and gratitude.

We strongly believe that it is very important for children to grow up in a positive environment, which is why we have created these books very carefully, introducing all the necessary tools for them to become grateful, confident, and open-minded.

If you find this book useful, you are more than welcome to explore our mindfulness book collection. Also, if you'd like to receive FREE self-development materials for your children and to receive notifications about our new releases, feel free to contact us.

Visit our website:
www.worldwide-creativity.com

Instagram:
https://instagram.com/worldwidecreativitypress

Facebook:
https://facebook.com/worldwidecreativitypress

A message for dad...

✦ This journal is fun and lighthearted, ✦ asking really good questions that will lead to great conversations that otherwise might be difficult to achieve with a teenager. Sometimes might be not so easy to open up, but with these carefully chosen prompts, it will be an absolutely fantastic way to record memories and encourage open communication with your children. The prompts are a great way to get the conversation going and are just deep enough to ask some serious questions without expecting too much of them. It switches back and forth between drawings and writing which is a good way to keep your daughter intrigued. Just use this journal to connect and listen and love your sweet daughter, learning and affirming who she is.

With love,

Worldwide Creativity

How to use this journal

Use your imagination, remember all the beautiful moments you went through, and don't think too much, it's not a logical journal, but a creative one. Play, be a child, color the images that can be colored, paste pictures where you can, and have fun with your daughter in this amazing journey of yours! Be passionate about what you write, share with your daughter all the great memories and allow yourself to make mistakes, proving to your daughter that mistakes happen and that's ok! Sharing this journal gives you both the opportunity to learn new things about each other and experience the emotions the other had.

You ❤ & ❤ Me

This is a picture or a drawing of us

WHAT DAY IS TODAY?

Date: _____

Today is the day we give birth to this journal, the day we will always remember fondly.

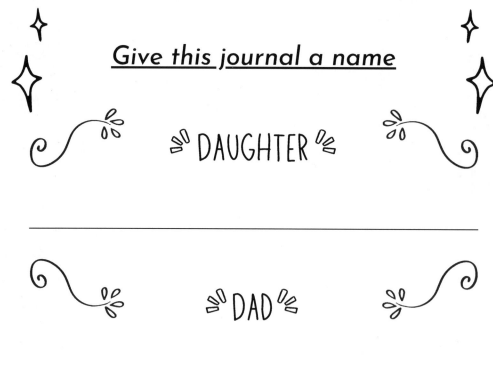

Give this journal a name

DAUGHTER

_____

DAD

_____

This will be your work of art. Take care of it, cherish it and enjoy it!

ALL ABOUT MY
DAD

(This is him)

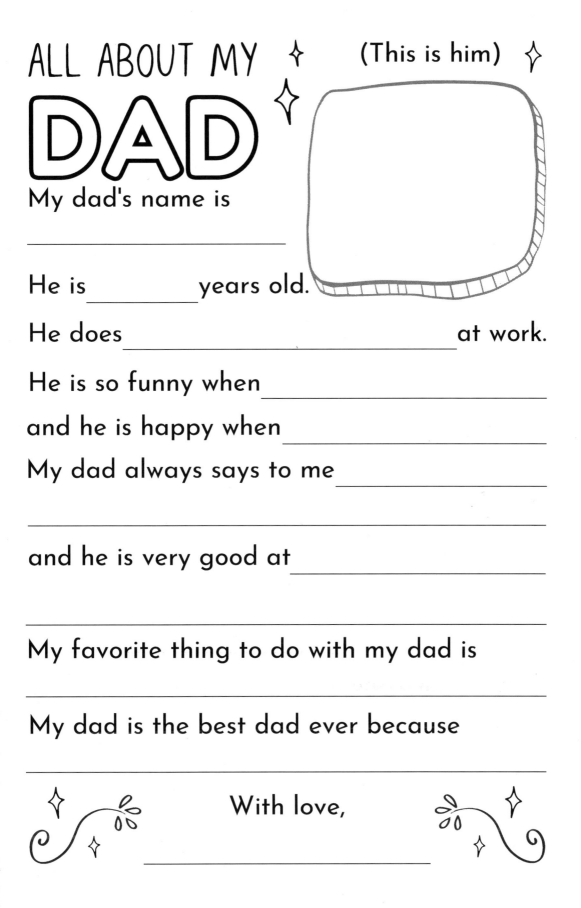

My dad's name is

_____

He is _____ years old.

He does _____ at work.

He is so funny when _____

and he is happy when _____

My dad always says to me _____

_____

and he is very good at _____

_____

My favorite thing to do with my dad is

_____

My dad is the best dad ever because

_____

With love,

_____

ALL ABOUT MY
Daughter

(This is a selfie of her)

My daughter's name is

_____

She is _____ years old.

She studies at _____

She is so funny when _____

and she is happy when _____

My daughter always says to me _____

_____

She is very good at _____

_____

My favorite thing to do with my daughter is

_____

•I love my daughter because

_____

With love,

_____

Personal Information

Date: _____

We live in:

_____

_____

We call each other:

_____

_____

Our eye color is:

_____

Our hair color is:

_____

_____

WRITE TOGETHER

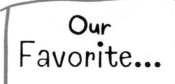

Our Favorite...

Date: _____

✏️ **Our favorite restaurant is:**

_____

_____

✏️ **Our favorite movie is:**

_____

_____

◇ **Our favorite game is:** ◇

_____

_____

Our favorite season is:

_____

_____

WRITE TOGETHER

Our Favorite...

Date: _____

Our favorite emoji is:

_____

_____

Our favorite sport is:

_____

_____

♢ Our favorite food is: ♢

_____

_____

♡ Our favorite place to visit is: ♡

_____

_____

WRITE TOGETHER

This is a picture or a drawing of our family

These are all of us

Their names and ages are:

_____

_____

_____

_____

Daughter writes

Date:

_____

DEAR DAD,

What are the three most important things in your life:

Dad writes

Date:

_____

DEAR DAUGHTER,

What are the three most important things in your life:

Daughter writes

Date:

DEAR DAD,

If you could give every person in the world one value, what would it be? What impact will have this value in society and what things can change for the better?

_____

_____

_____

_____

_____

_____

_____

_____

Dad writes

Date:

_____

DEAR DAUGHTER,

Colour the top five values that are most important for you:

Respect

Kindness   Trust   Fun

Saying sorry   Honesty

Friendship   Responsible

Helping others   Faith

Creativity   Happiness

Safety   Family   Patient

Being the best

Doing my best   Fairness

Popular

Being rich

School

Daughter writes

Date:
_____

DEAR DAD,

Did you have pets growing up? Tell me about them.

_____

_____

_____

What is the most embarrassing thing your mother or father ever did to you?

_____

_____

_____

What three adjectives would your grandparents use to describe you?

_____

_____

_____

Dad writes

Date:
_____

DEAR DAUGHTER,

Every year, our family celebrates:

_____
_____
_____

Special things our family do together:

_____
_____
_____

Interesting facts about our family:

_____
_____
_____

Your signature

Daughter writes

Date:

_____

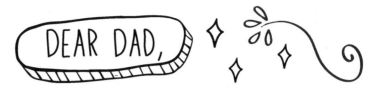
DEAR DAD,

What is the best thing your parents ever cooked?

_____

_____

_____

What's something your mom or dad used to tell you growing up that later turned out to be true?

_____

_____

_____

What was a favorite family tradition when you were growing up?

_____

_____

_____

Dad
writes

Date:
_____

DEAR DAUGHTER,

What do you know how to do that you can teach to others?

_____

_____

_____

If you could stop doing anything in your school day, what would it be?

_____

_____

_____

What was something you did that made you feel brave?

_____

_____

_____

Daughter
writes

Date:

_____

DEAR DAD,

Who was your best friend in elementary school? In high school?

_____

_____

_____

Did you ever win an award? What was it for?

_____

_____

_____

Do you like your name? Would you ever change it?

_____

_____

_____

Dad writes

Date:
_____

DEAR DAUGHTER,

What smell brings back a memory for you?
What is the memory?

_____
_____
_____

 What is your favorite
dessert?

_____
_____
_____

33. What was the worst thing you have ever
eaten? Why was it so bad?

_____
_____
_____

Daughter
writes

Date:

_____

DEAR DAD,

How did you feel about school, and what type of student were you?

_____

_____

_____

What songs have held special meaning to you over the years?

_____

_____

_____

What are the three happiest moments in your life so far?

_____

_____

_____

 Dad writes

Date:

_____

DEAR DAUGHTER,

What do you want to be when you grow up?

_____

_____

_____

What is your favorite place in the world?

_____

_____

_____

If you could invent something that would make life easier for people what would you invent?

_____

_____

_____

Daughter
writes

Date:
_____

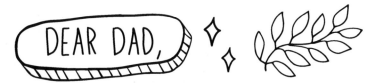

Who was the hero of your childhood? What did you like most about him?

_____

_____

_____

What was the first album or CD you ever bought and when did you buy it?

_____

_____

_____

Were you ever on any teams or play any sports?

_____

_____

_____

Dad writes

Date:

_____

What is your biggest worry?

_____

_____

_____

If you could meet a famous person, who would it be?

_____

_____

_____

If you could make one absolute rule for a day, what would it be?

_____

_____

_____

Daughter writes

Date:

_____

DEAR DAD,

How did you choose your career? What do you like most about it?

_____

_____

_____

What's the best gift you've ever received? What's the best gift you've ever given?

_____

_____

_____

Is there something you've always wanted to do or experience that you haven't had a chance to yet?

_____

_____

_____

Dad writes

Date:

_____

DEAR DAUGHTER,

What would life be like if no one had a
phone?

_____

_____

_____

If we had to leave today and you could only
bring one thing, what would you bring?

_____

_____

_____

If you could be any age for the rest of your
♢ life, what age would you be? Why? ♢

_____

_____

_____

Daughter
writes

Date:

_____

DEAR DAD,

What are you most proud of in life?

_____
_____
_____
_____

◇ What did you have as a child that kids today ◇
don't have?

_____
_____
_____

When do you feel the happiest?

_____
_____
_____
_____

Dad
writes

Date:

_____

 DEAR DAUGHTER,

What do you look forward to when you wake up every day?

_____

_____

_____

If only one of your toys could come alive and play with you, which one would it be?

_____

_____

_____

If you could be on a T.V. show, which one would it be?

_____

_____

_____

Daughter writes

Date:

_____

DEAR DAD,

✳ **What was the most difficult thing you went** ✳
through as a child?

How did you overcome it?

DAD WRITES

Date:

DEAR DAUGHTER,

_____

What is the most difficult thing you are going through now?

How do you overcome it? Do you need help?

DAUGHTER WRITES

Date:

_____

DEAR DAD,

What do you remember about when I was born?

How did you feel when you found out that you were going to be a father?

DAD WRITES

Date: _____

What is something that I do that makes you angry?

What is something that I do that makes you happy?

Date:

_____

What are your best memories of holidays or family gatherings as a child?

What is the best family reunion or family party that you remember attending as a child?

DAD WRITES

Date:

DEAR DAUGHTER,

_____

What is something that makes our family special?

If our whole family lived in a zoo, what kind of animals would each person be?

DAUGHTER WRITES

 Date:

 DEAR DAD,

How are you most like your parents? How are you different?

What do you remember most about being a teenager? What's your best advice for me?

 DAD WRITES

Date:

 ◇DEAR DAUGHTER,◇

_____

What is the funniest thing that ever happened to you?

If only one of your toys could come alive and play with you, which one would it be? Why?

 DAUGHTER WRITES

Date:

_____

DEAR DAD,

What are your memories about the houses you lived in as a kid? Did you have a favorite?

What do you think was the dumbest thing you did as a child?

DAD WRITES

Date:

_____

◇DEAR DAUGHTER,◇

Where would you like to visit if you could go anywhere?

If you could change your name, what would you name yourself? Why?

DAUGHTER WRITES

Date:

_____

What are the three happiest moments in your life so far?

Tell me about the three best decisions you've ever made.

Date:

_____

◇DEAR DAUGHTER,◇

What is the worst thing that has happened to you?

What did you learn from the worst thing that has happened to you?

DAUGHTER WRITES

Date:

_____

DEAR DAD,

What was the most difficult thing you went through as a child?

What lessons have you learned about other people in life?

DAD WRITES

Date:

_____

✧DEAR DAUGHTER,✧

Which sense is your favorite, seeing, hearing, tasting, smelling, or feeling? Why?

What is your favorite season? Why?

DAUGHTER WRITES

Date: _____

DEAR DAD,

What is the best advice your dad ever gave you?

Is there anything that you wish you had asked your parents but haven't/didn't?

Dad Writes

Date:

_____

What would you do if you could do anything you wanted?

What has been the best dream you ever had?

Date:
_____

If you could go back to one day in your childhood,
which day would that be? Why?

If you could time-travel, who would you visit and
why?

Date: _____

◇DEAR DAUGHTER,◇

If you were to give me a nickname, what would it be? Why?

If you wanted to make everyone on the planet smile, how would you do it?

DAUGHTER WRITES

Date:

What do you remember most about your wedding day?

What are your favorite things about my mother? "How did you meet?"

Date: _____

 ◇DEAR DAUGHTER,◇

If you could change any of the rules of this world, which ones would you change?

If you could change anything about your family what would it be?

  DAUGHTER WRITES

☆ Date: ☆
_____

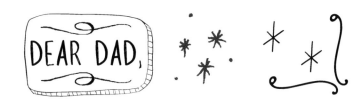

DEAR DAD,

\|/ Dad, what are your hopes for me? \|/

DAD WRITES

♡ Date: ♡

_____

DEAR DAUGHTER,

What do you think about my hopes for you?
Do they match your hopes? Would you like to
add or remove something?

DAUGHTER WRITES

 Date:

_____

DEAR DAD,

What relationship tips do you think have helped keep your friendships and romantic  relationships strong?

 DAD WRITES

DEAR DAUGHTER,

What do you wish we had more ability or time to do together? Tell me more about that.

 ☆ Date: ☆ DEAR DAD,
_____

Was there ever a moment with me where you wished you reacted differently and how so?

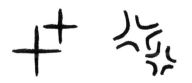  DAD WRITES

♡ Date: ♡ _____

(DEAR DAUGHTER,)

What is your biggest complaint about me?
✧ Tell me more about that. ✧

DAUGHTER WRITES

 Date:
_____

How did you prepare when you learned you
were going to have a daughter?

DEAR DAUGHTER,

What is something you never thought you could tell me but maybe want to tell me now?

☆ Date: ☆

_____

DEAR DAD,

How would you like to be remembered?

 DAD WRITES

♡ Date: ♡

_____

DEAR DAUGHTER,

What is your favorite thing about our relationship? Tell me more about that

DAUGHTER WRITES

☆ Date: ☆

_____

What's the biggest positive change you've seen in me over the years?

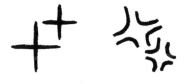  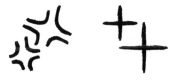

♡ Date: ♡ **DEAR DAUGHTER,**

_____

What's your biggest dream that you wish would come true?

 Date: ☆

_____

DEAR DAD,

Do you think I will accomplish my biggest dream? What advice do you have for me regarding my dream?

DAD WRITES

DEAR DAUGHTER,

If you could invent something to make life easier, what would you invent?

 Date:

_____

Why did you choose your career?

♡ Date: ♡ _____

DEAR DAUGHTER,

If you could pick one really nice thing to do for someone, what would it be and whom would it be for?

 Date:

_____

What do you admire most about your own father?

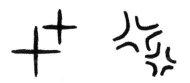  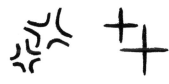

DEAR DAUGHTER,

If you got to be the parent for the day,
what rules would you have?

 Date:

_____

Do you think my rules are good enough? If not, please explain to me why.

♡ Date: ♡

_____

DEAR DAUGHTER,

What do you want your future to be like?

DAUGHTER WRITES

Date:

_____

What is the first thing you say to me in the morning?

_____

What is the last thing you say to me before bed?

_____

Date:

_____

What is the first thing you say to me in the morning?

_____

What is the last thing you say to me before bed?

_____

Date:

_____

 DEAR DAD,

How do I like you to call me?

_____

How do you like to call me?

_____

Date:

_____

 DEAR DAUGHTER,

How do I like you to call me?

_____

How do you like to call me?

_____

  WRITE TOGETHER

Date:

_____

If you had three wishes what would they be?

_____

_____

_____

Who do you think is the best actor/actress to play you in the movie about your life?

_____

Date:

_____

If you had three wishes what would they be?

_____

_____

_____

Who do you think is the best actor/actress to play you in the movie about your life?

_____

Date:

_____

Describe yourself using one word.

_____

Invent your own word. What does it mean?

_____

If you wrote a book, what would it be called?

_____

Date:

_____

Describe yourself using one word.

_____

Invent your own word. What does it mean?

_____

If you wrote a book, what would it be called?

_____

Date:

DEAR DAUGHTER,

_____

How would you spend your ideal day? Try to describe in as much detail as possible what a perfect day looks like for you.

DAUGHTER WRITES

Date:

DEAR DAD,

_____

How would you spend your ideal day? Try to describe in as much detail as possible what a perfect day looks like for you.

DAD WRITES

Date:

_____

DEAR DAUGHTER,

What's the hardest part about being a child?
Give me some examples you've been through.

DAUGHTER WRITES

Date:

_____

What's the hardest part about being a father? Give me some examples you've been through.

Date:

DEAR DAUGHTER,

_____

When was the last time you laughed really
hard and what was it about?

DAUGHTER WRITES

Date:

_____

 **DEAR DAD,**

When was the last time you laughed really hard and what was it about?

  DAD WRITES

Date:

_____

 DEAR DAUGHTER,

If you had to pick a theme song to describe you, what would it be?

When was the last time you felt really lucky that something good happened to you?

What is the biggest lesson you have ever learned?

   DAUGHTER WRITES

Date:

_____

 •DEAR DAD,•

What are three adjectives your friends use to describe you?

1

2

3

How would people who knew you in high school describe you?

What was your first job and how did it go?

  DAD WRITES

Date:

DEAR DAUGHTER,

What are **3** things your friends would say that you are really good at?

1

2

3

If you could be someone else for a day, who would you be? Why?

What is something you are not allowed to do, that you wish you could do?

DAUGHTER WRITES

Date:

 •DEAR DAD,•

_____

Are there things you wish you had done differently as a father?

Do you think today's fathers have things harder or easier than you had them?

What has been your favorite age so far, and why?

  DAD WRITES

Date:

_____

DEAR DAUGHTER,

What are you passionate about?

What are you thankful for?

Are you excited about your life? Is there
something you want to change?

DAUGHTER WRITES

Date:

DEAR DAD,

_____

What are the most amazing things we have done together?

1 _____

2 _____

3 _____

4 _____

Date:

DEAR DAUGHTER,

_____

What are the most amazing things we have done together?

1 _____

2 _____

3 _____

4 _____

WRITE TOGETHER

Date:

_____

DEAR DAD,

What amazing things we still have to do together?

1 _____

2 _____

3 _____

4 _____

Date:

_____

DEAR DAUGHTER,

What amazing things we still have to do together?

1 _____

2 _____

3 _____

4 _____

WRITE TOGETHER

FAVORITE THINGS

	DAUGHTER	DAD
Favorite Color		
Favorite Restaurant		
Favorite Fast Food		
Favorite Meal		
Favorite Flower		
Favorite Hobbie		
Favorite Candy		
Favorite Fruit		
Favorite Dessert		
Favorite Ice cream		
Favorite Snacks		
Favorite Drinks		
Favorite Book		
Favorite Game		

Date: _____

If you could design a new clothing line that everyone would wear, what would it look like? Draw your clothing line.

✦ Date: ✦

DEAR DAUGHTER,

If you could create a new color, how would it look, and what would you call it? Apply your new color to the images below.

The name of the color: _____

DAUGHTER DRAWS

✧ Date: ✧

_____

Do you have a favorite book? What's the name of the book? Draw your favorite book's cover below.

Your favorite book is: _____

DAUGHTER DRAWS

Date:
_____

Draw what happiness looks like to you. Use as many elements as you want, and use your imagination to the fullest.

  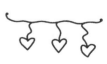

Date: _____

Draw yourself in the present moment.

Draw yourself ten years in the future.

DAUGHTER DRAWS

Date:

 **DEAR DAD,**

_____

What are your thoughts about my drawings above? How do you think it looks like?

What about my answers? Do you think they are good? If not, can you give some examples?

What do you think I need to improve based on how I did above?

   DAD WRITES

Date:
_____

 DEAR DAUGHTER,

What are three goals you have achieved so far?

 1

 2

 3

Do you have other goals you want to achieve? How can I help?

   DAUGHTER WRITES

Date:

 DEAR DAD,

_____

What do you think about my accomplishments?

What do you think about my other goals? Do you think I will achieve them?

   DAD WRITES

✧ **Date:** ✧

_____

DAD, I LOVE YOU BECAUSE YOU ARE...

Dear girl, color each word below that represents a quality of your daddy.

trustworthy

sympathetic

honest

smart

funny

hard-working

wise

supportive

loyal

patient

dedicated

strong

good listener

beautiful

humble

passionate

DAUGHTER WRITES

Date:

_____

 DEAR DAD,

What's something that I do that makes you proud of me?

What do you think are my best 5 qualities?

1

2

3

4

5

  DAD WRITES

Date:

DEAR DAD,

_____

What have YOU always wanted to ask ME?

My answer...

WRITE TOGETHER

Date:

What I love about you

Thanks to you, I believe I can

_____

Your kind words make me feel

_____

You are a great

_____

and a wonderful

_____

I really appreciate that you taught me

_____

The most important thing for me is that you

_____

 DAUGHTER WRITES

Date:

_____

DEAR DAUGHTER,

What was our most beautiful trip?

_____

_____

_____

The funniest picture we have of that trip.

DAUGHTER WRITES

Date:

_____

This is a picture of us being extremely happy!

Date:

_____

This is a picture of us making goofy faces.

Date:

This is a picture of us when we...

Date:

FINAL PICTURE

This is a picture of us when we finished this journal.

Date:

Dear Daughter,

Ohhh, we have reached the end of this journey.
What are your thoughts? Did you like this book?
Are you happy with our way to fill in?

What did you enjoy the most?

Now that we reached the end of this book,
what should we do next?

  DAUGHTER WRITES

Our Growth Mindset Collection Books for kids

With **50** + daily activities, affirmations and lessons, girls can build up their self-esteem and transform their sense of self! The mindfulness activities encourage girls to think beyond social conventions and inspire conversations with adults about what it really means to be confident, brave, and beautiful.

www.worldwide-creativity.com

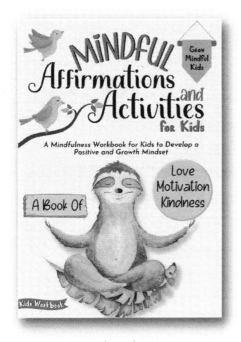

Change your child's mind-set in just a few minutes a day with the help of "Mindful Affirmations and Activities". This book contains three chapters that help children to manage their emotions, grow strong and confident. Mindful Affirmations, Mindful Coloring and Mindful Activities.

www.worldwide-creativity.com

This unique activity book helps young boys train their brains, increase confidence, develop coping skills, and handle tough situations. They'll learn to feel proud of who they are as they explore their intelligence, kindness, courage, and creativity. It is also designed to help boys explore what it means to be successful, brave, and confident.

www.worldwide-creativity.com

Boost Children's Confidence and Self-Esteem through Mindfulness Activities. Cultivating a Growth Mind-set is very important for kid's development. This book contains activities so that they can become more confident at school, with friends and, more importantly, with themselves.

www.worldwide-creativity.com

Thank You

As a small family business, your feedback is very important to us and we will appreciate it if you could take a little time to rate it on Amazon. This will be very helpful for us, the creators of the book, as well as for other customers to analyze the quality of the product.

We really hope you enjoy our work and find it really useful, fun, and easy for you and your daughter, and helps you to connect with each other and to strengthen your relationship.

We create our book with lots of love, but mistakes can always happen. If there are any issues with your book such as faulty bindings or printing errors, please contact the platform you purchased to obtain a replacement.

contact@worldwide-creativity.com

Worldwide
Creativity
Mindfulness

Can't wait to see you on **Instagram**

Instagram https://www.instagram.com/worldwidecreativitypress/

Qr-code

Can't wait to see you on **Facebook**

Facebook https://www.facebook.com/worldwidecreativitypress/

Qr-code

Visit our **Website**

Website https://worldwide-creativity.com/

Qr-code

Made in the USA
Las Vegas, NV
23 December 2024

15146297R00063